PASSPORT
GERMANY

Passport To The World

PASSPORT GERMANY

Your Pocket Guide to German Business, Customs & Etiquette

Roland Flamini

Passport Series Editor: Barbara Szerlip

WORLD TRADE PRESS®
Professional Books for International Trade

World Trade Press
1505 Fifth Avenue
San Rafael, California 94901 USA
Tel: (415) 454-9934
Fax: (415) 453-7980
E-mail: WorldPress@aol.com

"Passport to the World" concept: Edward G. Hinkelman
Cover design: Peter Jones, Marge Wilhite
Illustrations: Tom Watson

Passport GERMANY
Copyright © 1997 by World Trade Press. All Rights Reserved.

This publication is designed to provide general information con-
cerning the cultural aspects of doing business with people from a
particular country. It is sold with the understanding that the publisher is not engaged in rendering legal or any other professional
services. If legal advice or other expert assistance is required, the
services of a competent professional person should be sought.

Library of Congress Cataloging-in-Publication Data
Flamini, Roland
Passport Germany: your pocket guide to German business, customs & etiquette / Roland Flamini.
p. cm. -- (Passport to the world)
Includes bibliographical references.
ISBN 1-885073-20-8
1. Corporate culture -- Germany. 2. Business etiquette -- Germany.
3. Negotiation in business -- Germany. 4. Intercultural communi-
cation. I. Title. II. Series.
HD58.7.F58 1996
390' .00943--dc21
96-49110 CIP

Printed in the United States of America

Table of Contents

GERMANY

Europe's Economic Giant

Germany
Quick Look

Official name	Bundesrepublik Deustsch-land
Land area	355,744 sq km (137,352 sq mi)
Capital & largest city	Berlin
People	
Population	81,087,506
Annual growth (1995)	0.36%
Official language	German
Major religions	Protestant 45%, Roman Catholic 37%, other 18%
Economy	
GDP (1996)	US$1,351 trillion US$16,700 per capita
Foreign trade	Imports—US$373.6 billion Exports—US$392 billion Surplus—US$18.4 billion
Principal trade partners	European Union 51.3% France 11.0% Netherlands 9.2% EFTA 13.3% United States 6.8%
Currency	Deutschemark
Exchange rate (2/97)	1.64 DM = US$1
Education and health	
Literacy (1996)	99%
Universities (1989)	54
Life expectancy (1995)	Female—79 years; Male—73 years
Infant mortality (1996)	6.2 deaths/1,000 live births

GERMANY

Country Facts

Geography and Demographics

The Federal Republic of Germany is the third largest country in Europe after France and Spain. It borders on France and the Netherlands in the southwest, Poland and the Czech Republic in the east, Denmark to the north, and Austria and Switzerland in the south. Its 2,389 kilometers of coastline principally border the North Sea. There are four geographical zones: the broad lowlands of the north, the central uplands, the valleys of the Rhine River in the south and west, and in the south, bordering on Switzerland, the Alps and the Black Forest. Its population is one third that of the entire United States, though its size is comparable to the state of Montana.

Climate

The climate is temperate and marine. Summer temperatures don't usually rise above 29°C (85°F), and there are occasional warm, tropical *Foehn* winds. The winters are cold, with high rainfall and high relative humidity. The south can receive large amounts of snow. Germany's varied terrain is ideal for hiking, a favorite national activity.

Business Hours

From 9 A.M. to 5 or 5:30 P.M. Monday through Friday is standard. Some businesses tend to start and finish earlier (8 A.M. to 4 P.M. or 7:30 A.M. to 3:30 P.M.), which has advantages in winter when darkness falls very early. Banks are open weekdays from 9 A.M. to 3 P.M. Store hours are from 9 A.M. to 5 or 6:30 P.M., and until 2 P.M. on Saturday (except one Saturday each month when they remain open into the evening). In some areas, stores (other than department stores) close for one hour at noon.

National Holidays

Neujahr (New Year's Day) . . . . January 1
> An old tradition calls for the eating of carp or pork with sauerkraut on this day.

Karfreitag (Good Friday) . . . . . . March/April
Ostersonntag und Ostermontag
(Easter Sunday & Monday) . . . . March/April
Pfingsten (Pentecost) . . . . May/June
> Honors the Holy Spirit descending on Christ's apostles

Christi Himmelfahrt
(Ascension Thursday) . . . . May/June
> Honors Christ's ascent to Heaven (40 days after Easter)

Tag der Arbeit (Labor Day) . . . May 1
> Honors workers with parades, dances and parties

Tag der Deutschen Einheit
(Day of German Unity) . . . . October 3
> Marks the 1990 reunification of the two Germanys

Allerheiligen (All Saints' Day) . . November 1
Repentance Day . . . . November
(varies)
> Day of national atonement for World War II

Weihnachten (Christmas) . . . . . December 24-26
Sylvester (New Year's Eve) . . . . December 31

Regional Holidays

Heilige Drei Könige
(Feast of the Epiphany) . . . . . . January 6

> Celebrates visit of the three kings to the Christ child;
> only observed in Bavaria and Baden-Württemberg.

Fronleichnam
(Corpus Christi) . . . . First Sunday
in June

> Observed with open-air masses and processions carry-
> ing the Eucharist through the streets.

Maria Himmelfahrt
(Feast of the Assumption) . . . . August 15

> Celebrates Mary's ascension to Heaven; in Bavaria and
> Saarland

Reformationstag
(Reformation Day) . . . . October 31

> Celebrates Martin Luther's Reformation movement; in
> former East Germany

(For more on holidays, see Chapter 16: Customs.)

2   The Germans

Language

German is spoken by more Europeans than any other language (and it's one of the few languages in the world in which all nouns begin with a capital letter). In addition to being the mother tongue of 85 million Germans, it's spoken in Austria and parts of Switzerland, by some people in the Alsace-Lorraine region of France, in Luxembourg, and by large German minorities in central Europe. It's almost two languages — Low German (*Plattdeutsch*, spoken in the north) and High German (*Hochdeutsch*), the latter being the literary language generally used by writers and upscale newspapers.

Traditionally, German was written in *Fraktur*, an elaborate Gothic style that dates back to the 14th century. However, after World War II, *Fraktur* was largely replaced by Roman characters. The only diacritical mark is the umlaut, two small dots that appear over the letters *ä*, *ö* and *ü*.

"An average sentence in a German newspaper ... occupies a quarter of a column ... it is built mainly of compound words constructed by the writer, and not to be found in the dictionary, [words that] ... treat fourteen or fifteen different subjects, each enclosed in a parenthesis of its own," wrote American author Mark Twain. "Finally all the parentheses and re-parentheses are massed together between a couple of king-parentheses, one of which is placed in the first line of the majestic sentence and the other in the middle of the last line of it — *after* which comes THE VERB and you find out for the first time what the man has been talking about."

Like many who try to learn the language, Twain was baffled by its complexity and what he called its "alphabetical processions" (long composite words "compacted into one without joint or seam"). Sentence word order is strictly regulated, with the verb generally coming at the end, as it does in Latin.

More than most tongues, German reflects the national character of those who speak it. A commitment to order — *Ordnung* — dominates German life. *Alles in Ordnung* (Everything is as it should be) is both a constantly heard phrase and a state of being. Composite words may be clumsy and prosaic, but they satisfy the Germans' desire for precision and clarity. The German word for glove is *Handschuh*; language doesn't get more literal than that.

This quest for clarity extends to pronunciation. No matter how long and guttural, German words are pronounced as written, without any of the tricky peculiarities of English and French. What you see is what you say.

German words that have been incorporated into English include *sauerkraut, hamburger, pumpernickel, kindergarten, dachshund, poodle, lager, ersatz, edelweiss, wanderlust, wunderkind, hinterland, blitzkrieg* and *meerschaum*. (*Meer* means "sea" and *schaum* "foam," as the white mineral from which these pipes are carved — often in the shape of animals, devils or people — was once thought to be petrified sea foam.) The American military term *flak*, as in anti-aircraft fire, is a contraction of the

German words *Flieger* (aviator), *Abwehr* (defense) and *Kanonen* (guns).

The Germans acknowledge that theirs is a difficult language, so non-Germans who speak it well go up several notches in their estimation. A surprising number of West German executives are fluent enough in English to conduct business negotiations in it without an interpreter. East Germans are more likely to speak Russian as a second language, but since reunification, the younger generation has lost no time in switching to English courses. (For information on regional dialects, see Chapter 4.)

The Burden of History

The atrocities of Hitler's Third Reich cast an indelible shadow over the country. Many Germans are ambivalent about their wartime past. Part of the Nazi legacy is a strong distrust of authority (in contrast to the traditional German faith in it) and of the military, a distrust that has led members of the younger generation to favor pacifism. Many are members of Amnesty International and Greenpeace. German painter Gottfried Helnwein has gained international renown for his chilling anti-Fascist and anti-militarist canvases.

Though a member of NATO, Germany spent decades refusing to allow its armed forces to serve outside its borders, in order to avoid stirring up wartime memories. In 1996, after an acrimonious debate in the *Bundestag* (Parliament), the government finally agreed to join the NATO force in Bosnia-Herzegovina.

The burden of recent history helps explain the central German paradox: On the one hand, their country is the fourth richest in the world, their economy is the locomotive for the European Union (EU), and their goods have a reputation for high quality and dependability. Under its system of government by consensus — the cornerstone of Germany's postwar prosperity — employers and unions cooperate in the management of companies. Worker-directors sit on the boards of the major corporations. Pay and conditions are set across whole industries through negotiation between union and managerial representatives, and change is put into effect in small steps.

On the other hand, the German people remain deeply insecure. Angst, the feeling of vulnerability to life's uncertainties, is a national trait. Germans tend to overreact, particularly when their orderly world is threatened. In a recent radio program, one political analyst in Frankfurt likened the present situation in Germany to the dawn of the French Revolution: "You feel that this state is nearing some kind of bankruptcy," he declared.

But in fact, Germany's economy remains the sturdiest in Europe. What's happening is that faced with slowing growth and rising unemployment, coupled with the financial burden of rebuilding the East, the government has planned cutbacks in Germany's model (and very expensive) social welfare system, the so-called Welfare Net. (For background on this, see Chapter 6.) This has triggered alarm bells. The notion that the paternalistic state (the Fatherland) can no longer guarantee that every citizen will be looked after from the cradle to the grave has brought protests from the labor unions and increasing angst to the populace at large.

Reunification: Fleeting Euphoria

Another source of economic pressure is something many Germans dreamed of, but few expected to happen: Reunification.

In the immediate aftermath of World War II,

the defeated Third Reich was divided into a pro-West Federal Republic and a Soviet satellite state, the so-called Democratic Republic. Viewed as fitting retribution in some Allied quarters, the division caused families to split up, many people to be uprooted, and a new European balance of power to be created. "The idea that one day a state of 75 million Germans could [again] arise in the middle of Europe arouses concern in many of our neighbors and partners in Europe," admitted Chancellor Helmut Schmidt as recently as 1979. (Schmidt also compared the division to splitting the U.S. state of Oregon — roughly the same size of Germany — into two separate states.)

In 1989, following the collapse of the East German regime and the fall of the Berlin Wall, the dream of reunification suddenly became a reality. Though it was a welcome event, the marriage quickly ran into domestic problems. West Germans were suddenly confronted with the high cost of cementing together two nations, one of which was riddled with the flaws resulting from 45 years of communist rule — infrastructure in bad shape, inefficient and vastly overstaffed factories, and wages climbing faster than productivity, augmented by massive environmental disasters. Seventeen million more people now had to be absorbed into the country's workforce and social welfare system.

Germany Now

Eight years after Leonard Bernstein's triumphant conducting of Beethoven's Ninth Symphony on the site of the just-demolished Berlin Wall, the process of reunification remains a complex mixture of promise and disappointment.

Though the federal government is scheduled to move to Berlin from Bonn in the year 2000, Berlin has already assumed the role of integrated Germany's new capital, if not the capital of all of Eastern Europe. The city is in the middle of a massive construction boom — the skyline a forest of cranes, the eastern landscape awash in construction sites and earth movers. Money is pouring in from both private investors (mainly German) and the government, pumping new energy and vitality into local businesses. Friedichstrasse, once the drab main street of East Berlin, is now an avenue of stylish storefronts offering every designer label imaginable. There's also a thriving club scene. Reconstruction on an ambitious scale is also surging in other major eastern cities like Leipzig, where American-style shopping malls are the rage.

On the downside, there's the worrisome undertow of East Germany's economic collapse. The closing of many bankrupt factories and businesses has pushed unemployment nationwide to 12 percent, the highest recorded since the 1930s. Unemployment in the east is around 15 percent, and that's not counting the East Germans engaged in government make-work programs.

The anxiety-prone Germans are deeply concerned about the interlocking series of resentments that economic stagnation is producing. West Germans (or *Wessis*, as they're now called) regard East Germans as idle and complaining and an unwelcome burden. Many East Germans (*Ossis*), for their part, feel like second-class citizens. Germans are, in effect, one nation but two peoples. And it's not just economic pressure that's prolonging the alienation. What initially appeared to be gaps in language, culture and expectations turned out to be wide gulfs that may take a couple of generations to bridge.

Nostalgia for the Wall

By the spring of 1993, polls showed that 85 percent of the *Ossis* no longer felt happy about reunification — a significant jump from the almost 100 percent approval rate three years earlier. (By 1996, that percentage would drop to about 51 percent.) One East German joke was: "Why do most Chinese smile all the time?" Answer: "Because they still have their Wall." A typical *Ossi* lament was: "We used to have some money but no goods to spend it on. Now there are plenty of goods, but we have no money."

With the government pouring about US$150 billion annually into the eastern provinces (mostly for public works and infrastructure), Bonn's debt — accrued from its unification initiative — mounted astronomically. For Germans from the east, it wasn't just the pressure to increase productivity (one third of the west's in 1994) or even the rising crime rate. ("The real reason East Germany didn't have too many robberies in the old days," went another joke, "was that you had to wait 18 years for a getaway car.") The challenge was (and is) to accept the notion that East Germany is now part of an increasingly integrated Western European community with Atlantic ties, rather than part of a Moscow-dominated Eastern European strategic bloc.

And young East Germans are coming face to face, for the first time, with the western version of Germany's role in World War II. While the country's 16 federal states exercise independent authority over their school curriculums, they're required by law to provide a full accounting of the Nazi era and the Holocaust. Students are suddenly discovering that Jews, not Communists, were the principal victims at Buchenwald and other concentration camps. And able to travel freely for the first time, those same youths are finding out firsthand that the

United States isn't a quagmire of decadent capital-
ism, as they'd been taught.

In 1997, after a year of debate, and in an effort
to lure tourists, the government gave its approval
for a 20 kilometer (12 mile) red stripe to be painted
through the heart of Berlin, marking where the Wall
once stood. For many former East Berliners, however, the stripe is an offensive reminder of the ways
in which the city still remains divided. The plan is
to replace the stripe with a more permanent row of
inlaid marker stones when funds allow.

How Germans View Themselves

"The Germans," said renowned German poet
and dramatist Johann Wolfgang von Goethe (1749-
1832), "make everything difficult, both for themselves and for everyone else." If complexity didn't
exist, the Germans would have invented it. They
see themselves as a complex people living in an
intricate, untidy world that needs to be constantly
put in order. Karl Friedrich Moser, the 18th-century
writer and publisher, put it this way: "Every nation
has its principal motive. In Germany, it is obedi-
ence; in England, freedom; in Holland, trade; in
France, the honor of the king."

The Germans are rational, disciplined, efficient
and industrious, but they have another side, too — a
romantic one that allows them to escape into what the
poet Heinrich Heine called "the airy realm of
dreams." Germany's main river, the Rhine, has
inspired a rich Gothic folklore about singing maidens
(Wagner immortalized them in his opera cycle *The
Ring of the Nibelungen*) luring ships to destruction on
the rocky shore. The country's legendary heroes, such
as Siegfried and Lohengrin, are knights in shining
armor who kill dragons and save young virgins (who,
despite their gratitude, then marry someone else).

Germans flock to the Bavarian Coach Tour, a three-day trip in a circa-1830 mail coach drawn by horses through lush woodlands to "Mad" King Ludwig's 19th-century fantasy castle at Neu-schwanstein. As the horses canter past snow-covered pine trees and beside elegant lakes, the Germany of the *Autobahn* seems very far away. Nothing quite like this romantic tour (which starts and ends in Munich) exists elsewhere in Europe.

The melding of rational and romantic is evident in the choice of such national historical heroes as King Frederick the Great (1712-1786), who combined military genius with a talent for flute playing and composing, and aviator Baron Manfred von Richthofen, the infamous (and dashing) "Red Baron" of World War I.

Longing For The Beyond

This innate romanticism is also reflected in the belief that one's destiny can only be truly fulfilled far from familiar surroundings. So it's not surprising that Germans are relentless tourists. (The English word *wanderlust*, coined in 1902, has German roots.) Before reunification, West Germans used to make 90 million vacation trips a year, about half of them abroad. East Germans also feel *Fernweh* (a longing for the beyond), but under Communism, their travel was restricted to such "fraternal" vacation spots as Havana and Leningrad.

This enthusiasm for travel is a sign of affluence, but it's also an expression of a restless national character (which, combined with a love of nature, has resulted in a preponderance of German hiking clubs). The 19th-century poet Gustav Freytag believed that German wanderlust "ultimately expresses the search for an ideal country." Being perfectionists, Germans are still looking — in the

Mediterranean, in the Caribbean, on safari in Africa, and even at California's Disneyland. Recently, a German newspaper columnist noted that such globe-trotting only serves to confirm his countrymen's Germanness. They demand (and get) *Schnitzel* and *Wurst* on five continents, and they get up at dawn to be sure of securing the best places on the beach.

Ever resourceful, the Germans have even found a way to indulge their wanderlust without even having to cross a border. Inspired in large part by the works of Karl May — a 19th-century writer who never set foot in the U.S. but nevertheless churned out a hugely popular series of novels featuring a fictional Apache brave named Winnetou — approximately 85,000 Germans from suburban Hamburg to rural Bavaria spend their weekends in eagle-feathered headdresses and embroidered buckskins, acting out May's romanticized accounts of Native Americans. Engineers and advertising executives live in tepees, gather around campfires to eat buffalo meat (imported from Poland), and perform snake dances to the rhythm of American Indian chants.

It's One World, an environmentally correct clothing line (everything is biodegradable, no chlorine dyes used), takes a more philanthropic approach. Founded in 1992 by Britta Steilmann, daughter of the owner of Germany's largest textile company, It's One World uses some of its profits to improve conditions halfway around the world — for Dakota Sioux living on the Pine Ridge Reservation in the state of South Dakota.

A Country of Do's and (Mostly) Don'ts

Ordnung manifests itself in a welter of rules and regulations. The most minute aspects of daily life are controlled by some law or other. Throughout Germany, noise of any kind is *verboten* (forbidden) during "quiet time" — between 1:30 and 3:30 in the afternoon. (Back in the 1820s, when harmonicas, accordions and concertinas became the rage in European music, many Germans became so outraged at the resulting cacophony that they burned thousands of those instruments in public fires.) Mowing the lawn on Sunday afternoon breaks two laws: the one barring manual labor on Sunday and the one prohibiting noise.

Some years ago, a German court ruled that the horses belonging to a cavalry unit of the British Army stationed on a NATO base in Germany had to be licensed as means of transport. The license numbers subsequently hung from the horses' tails when they were used on ceremonial occasions. In 1990, postal worker representatives spent four days wrangling with the Deutsche Bundespost (the postal service) over the length of the *Pinkelpause* — the hourly bathroom break. The union didn't consider two minutes seventeen seconds long enough and held out, successfully, for four minutes.

A recent example of the "things as they should be" principle in action was the widely publicized court suit initiated by a German family who had gone on vacation in Turkey. In the final week of their three-week stay, ten handicapped people confined to wheelchairs were also visiting their hotel. Back home in Germany, the family sued their travel agency and won a 10 percent refund, plus court costs. The judge ruled that the sight of so many disabled persons "during every meal caused nausea and was an incessant and unusually strong reminder of human suffering. Such an experience is not what is typically expected from holidays."

Two areas of personal freedom are the *Autobahns* (few have speed limits) and the absence of nonsmoking regulations. It's been posited that driving fast is the German outlet for aggression. Smoking more or less where they please is another small act of independence. When Lufthansa tried to introduce nonsmoking flights on its domestic routes, no scheduled trip being longer than 90 minutes, the announcement caused such a public outcry that the airline hastily reversed its decision.

Attitudes Toward Other Cultures

Germans find the Italians excitable and hopelessly inefficient and the French arrogant, and they sometimes refer to the Dutch as "cheeseheads." Polls show that the European Union country they most admire is Britain.

Many Germans view Americans as inadequately educated, culturally shallow workaholics who don't know how to balance their jobs with leisure. Still, Germans are drawn to American popular culture, they admire the American entrepreneurial spirit, and they acknowledge the U.S. as a superpower. Since 1991, German direct investment in the U.S. has increased by 60 percent, and some German companies (notably Siemens) have even transplanted their apprenticeship (job training) programs to American high schools.

National Identity and Pride

Classical music has received its finest interpretation from the Berlin Philharmonic under the baton of its long-time resident conductor, Herbert von Karajan. In Munich, Karl Stockhausen pioneered electronic composition. Novelist Günter Grass shaped the writing of his generation. Jil

Sander, Karl Lagerfield and Hugo Boss have achieved international fame as fashion designers. Baron Heinrich von Thyssen's name has become a byword not for his family's steel company but for his vast contemporary art collection.

Germans attach major importance to *Bildung* (education and culture). The *Abitur*, the demanding national examination taken by high school seniors that can gain them entry into quality universities, requires young Germans to have read (and understood) Immanuel Kant's 18th-century *Critique of Pure Reason*, as well as the works of Goethe, Shakespeare and others. Virtually all under-20s in Germany are still full-time students.

Much of German history is also a source of pride. German literature dates all the way back to 800 B.C. with the heroic poem "Song of Hildebrand." Johann Gutenberg (1390-1468) created one of the most important inventions of Western civilization, a printing press with movable type, and the world's first printed book was a German bible.

Germany has given the world Richard Wagner and the four Bachs (Johann Sebastian, Carl Philipp Emanuel, Johann Christian and Wilhelm Friedemann), Wolfgang Amadeus Mozart and Ludwig van Beethoven, Friedrich Nietzsche, Martin Luther, Frederich von Schiller and Thomas Mann, as well as Lotte Lenya and Marlene Dietrich. (For information on German cinema, see Chapter 20.)

German-born Ludwig Mies van der Rohe was an architectural genius of the 1920s (perhaps best known for his credo "Less is more"). His contemporary, Walter Gropius, founded the Bauhaus, a school of design whose distinct aesthetic — a synthesis of early-20th-century technology and Old-World craftsmanship — continues to have worldwide influence today.

3 Cultural Stereotypes

Plodding Teutons

Germans take everything at face value.

Germans sometimes mistake diplomacy or subtlety for insincerity. And the tactic, often used by Americans, of first saying something positive and then following it up with a criticism leaves them confused. Are they being complimented or criticized? The old joke — that if a German is asked, "Do you know the time?" he or she will reply, "Yes, I do" (end of discussion) — illustrates the importance of being specific in conversation with them.

Taking things literally and being direct go hand in hand, and the Germans are remarkably direct when it comes to issues of sexuality. Brothels are legal, and major cities have red light districts. The most famous is Hamburg's (pre-AIDS) *Reeperbahn*, where women sit at their windows in various stages of undress waiting for clients. Both sexes frequent sex clubs — there's one at Frankfurt Airport — and discuss sexual topics with the same frankness with which they talk about automobiles and restaurant menus.

Overly Cautious

Germans are unwilling to take risks.

They're more wary than unwilling. Chancellor Helmut Kohl's party, the Christian Democrats, first came to power after World War II with the election slogan, "No experiments."

Germans strive for consensus and maximum stability. Contemporary political rhetoric reflects this determination to not rock the boat. *Friede* (peace) has several derivatives, such as the all-important *Sozialer Friede* (social peace) and the labor term *Friedenspflicht* (the obligation to maintain peace, as in the banning of wildcat strikes). Also frequently heard are *Normalisierung* (normalization), *Ausgleich* (balance or compromise), *Dialog* (dialogue), *Sozialpartnerschaft* (social partnership), *Mitte* (mainstream or middle road), *Kontinuität* (continuity), *Verlässlichkeit* (reliability) and *Geborgenheit* (a cross between shelter and warmth). *Geborgenheit* was what East Germans had — and some miss — in the so-called Democratic Republic.

The German expression *die Qual der Wahl* — the torture of choosing — also suggests a preference for clearly defined parameters and limited options.

This caution extends to the way Germans manage their money. The German stock exchange barely exists, and few individuals invest in equities the way Americans do. Preferred is the so-called *Pfundebriefe*, a super-safe, low-interest, real-estate-backed mortgage security that's widely considered the "Fort Knox" of German investment.

Arrogant

Germans have a very high opinion of themselves.

Germans hate making mistakes, and they *really* hate admitting to them. When they're in the wrong, their reaction is to become aggressive. They also set great store by frankness, living by the conviction that plain speaking may make them sound tactless or brutal, but at least it's honest. And they expect others to follow suit, even though they may not always like what they hear.

Overly Serious

Germans have no sense of humor.

Germans have plenty of humor, but they prefer organized burlesque to spontaneous levity. They seldom have enough self-confidence to laugh at themselves. Joke telling is a popular ritual associated with drinking, and the Germans tend to be very good raconteurs.

During the pre–Easter Carnival, Germans don colorful costumes, wear masks or paint their faces. (For more on this, see Chapter 16: Customs.) Birthdays are another occasion for sending jokey messages and poems. Political cabarets, a postwar institution, have millions of ardent fans.

Variety shows on German television are a bawdy mix of musical numbers and slapstick humor. A dubbed version of the 1960s American TV series "Hogan's Heroes" — which pokes fun at life in a World War II German prisoner-of-war camp — is popular, particularly among younger viewers, igniting a spark of hope that they may be more capable of seeing the humorous side of life than their elders. There's even a German-language "Hogan's Heroes" home page on the Internet.

4   Regional Differences

Germany isn't nearly as homogeneous as is generally believed. Once an amalgam of independent principalities, it's now a federation of *Länder* (regions), each with wide autonomy — except in the areas of foreign policy, defense and internal security. Regional characteristics and traditions are often a source of pride and are jealously defended.

The Bavarians tell jokes about the stiffness of the Prussians. Both make jokes about the cunning of the Saxons and the quick wit of Berliners. Saxons and Thuringians are said to be self-reliant entrepreneurs, and eastern Pomeranians are noted for their lack of industrial initiative.

Dialects: Alive and Well

Regional language differences flourish, despite commentators' laments that television is killing them. Each state has its own dialect, and even the speech of highly educated Germans is influenced by them.

Most dialects derive from either Swabian, Bavarian, Franconian or Plattdeutsch. Natives of Hamburg (Anglophiles all) regard the German spoken in Bavaria as barbarous; the Bavarians return the compliment. Variations range from different inflections to different words. Thus, the standard German greeting *Guten Tag* (Good day) becomes *Grüss Gott* (Greetings, literally "Greet God") in Bavaria. And while a woman in the north may be addressed simply as *Frau*, in the south she would be called *Gnädige Frau* (Gentle lady).

However, dialects have little effect on business. Major corporations, with branches all over the country, have introduced their own brand of nationalism, moving executives according to corporate needs, and thereby diluting the company's regional element in any given location. Also, in order to appeal to national market forces, companies look for common ground when it comes to selling their products.

Regional Fare

There are literally thousands of local dishes or local variations of dishes. Among them are:

- **Labskaus**. Originally a fisherman's breakfast, it's a hash of beef brisket, herring, beets, potatoes and salted pickles, served with a fried egg on top.
- **Weisswürste**. These white sausages of veal and herbs are boiled and eaten with sweet mustard.
- **Leberkäse**. Though it means "liver cheese," this Bavarian specialty is actually a steamed, crunchy crusted pork loaf served with mustard and sauerkraut.
- **Grünkohl mit Pinkel.** From Bremen comes this winter dish of steamed kale mixed with bits of pork belly, bacon and a very fatty sausage.

Government & Business

Consensus Politics in Action

After World War II, the German economy was in a shambles and dependent on Allied aid. In 1948, Economics Minister (and later Chancellor) Ludwig Erhard launched the *Soziale Marktwirtschaft*, a bold plan that abolished the rationing of essential goods, removed price and wage controls (introduced by the Nazis and kept in force by the Allied Occupying Powers), reformed the currency, and slashed tariffs on imported goods, thereby slowing down inflation and forcing German manufacturers to be more competitive.

As devised by Erhard, the system combines the principles of a free-market economy with an elaborate social security program (health insurance, free medical care, and unemployment and old age benefits). An income tax schedule that bears down heavily on all classes of society keeps prices in balance, but at the same time creates tax incentives that boost productivity.

The interests of business, government and society, as well as of management and labor, are presumed to be the same. This culture of cooperation (or *Mitbestimmungsrecht*) is designed to avoid the recurrent union confrontations that have plagued market economies in other Western countries. Workers are brought into the decision-making process in German corporations, and union representatives into the boardroom to run those corporations. In the health system, for example, German doctors and insurers quietly agree to reasonable rates, keeping customer costs relatively in check.

There's general agreement that German competitiveness is being undermined by the astronomical cost of labor and that any solution to the country's current economic ills must include reform of the welfare state. But despite much discussion, there's still no consensus on how to go about rectifying things. The federal government, unused to confrontation, seems to lack the political will to take the bull by the horns. The Social Democrat opposition and the unions, meanwhile, are insisting that any reforms be "socially just." So while a deal will probably be made eventually, the road to it is going to be difficult.

Help for Exporters

The closeness of government and business is best seen in the export field. As domestic demand and investment slowed down in the 1980s, German manufacturers stepped up exports and the Federal government backed them all the way. Government support takes the form of credit guarantees through Hermes Gmbh., the German export credit bank. In high-risk markets, German manufacturers and contractors can receive up to 100 percent government guarantees — giving them a distinct competitive edge over other foreign exporters who often have to seek financing in private sector banking.

The country's specialization in investment goods such as cars, machinery and industrial equipment allowed it to profit considerably from the world economic buoyancy of the second half of the 1980s. In recent years, high prices have eroded Germany's position as the world's number one exporter, but per capita, Germany still sells four times as much abroad as the U.S. and more than twice as much as Japan.

Rabattgesetz

Domestically, Germany's free-market economy is limited by such higher considerations as "fairness" and the sacrosanctity of weekends and evenings. Retail competition is regulated by *Rabattgesetz*, a federal law that requires stores in the same area to coordinate price reductions, so that sales people don't become involved in anything as undignified as a sales war and consumers don't waste their time shopping around for the best buys. The Center for the Combatting of Unfair Competition forbids advertisers to make direct comparisons with competitors or to offer anything as "free."

Rabattgesetz also puts strict limitations on shopping hours. Stores are not allowed to stay open after 6:30 P.M. on weekdays or after noon on Saturdays. There's also some fear that any move toward American-style, 24-hour, seven-days-a-week shopping may disrupt family activities and ultimately erode family values. This system is particularly hard on working women and single/divorced men, who have no choice but to shop before they go to work, during their lunch breaks, or on Saturday mornings.

Efforts to expand shopping hours (encouraged by the presence of such foreign retailers as Blockbuster Video, Gap, Inc. and Toys "R" Us) have met with sharp resistance from retail workers' unions, as well as from small retail outlets, who argue that hiring shift workers isn't practical.

A Welter of Regulations

As Germany is a member of the European Union, protective tariffs against the importation of foreign goods aren't allowed. Still, tough German regulations controlling domestic production keep many would-be foreign imports off the shelves. Products must conform to any of the more than 40,000 regulations and standards governing their manufacture and content, as well as to more than 25,000 other "norms" compiled by DIN, the national standards agency.

It's important to know, going in, which standards apply to your product and to obtain timely testing and certification. The organization responsible for testing technical or mechanical products and issuing the necessary certificate is the *Technischer Überwachungsverein e.V* (TÜV). TÜVs are private companies set up by each state; many have offices in other European countries and in the United States, and there's one in Japan.

While the welter of regulations may be discouraging, it's not impenetrable, says Leo Welt, head of the Washington-based German-American Business Council. "If you want to be in Germany, you work your way through them," he says. "It takes time because they cover many important areas. For instance, there are a lot of safety regulations." The presence of many American and other foreign manufacturers shows that it's possible to establish a foothold in Europe's biggest single national market. Procter & Gamble, a longtime presence in the Federal Republic, did more than US$3 billion worth of business in Germany in 1996.

Other firmly established U.S. companies include Kraft Foods, General Motors and Avis. A marketing expert in Frankfurt singled out the launch of Milky Way candy bars by the Mars Company as a successful campaign by a foreign manufacturer to sell in Germany. Germany is also an important market for U.S. horticultural products. In 1993, American exports of citrus, raisins, prunes, almonds, etc. reached $300 million.

CDU, SPD, CSU & The Greens

Since the 1950s, the pendulum of political power in West Germany has swung between two major parties, Konrad Adenauer's (and now Helmut Kohl's) Christian Democratic Union (CDU) and the Social Democratic Party (SPD) of Willy Brandt and Helmut Schmidt. But Germany's complex proportional electoral system — which favors small parties — consistently robbed both major political groups of an absolute majority, thereby turning two smaller parties into minor, but indispensable, coalition partners.

The Bavarian right-wing Christian Social Union (CSU), the CDU's traditional parliamentary ally, was led by Franz Josef Strauss, a flamboyant, saber-rattling, anti-Soviet rhetorician who wore Bavarian lederhosen (leather shorts) and whose favorite term for the SPD was "a party of traitors." The SPD relied on support from the liberal Free Democrats, whose leading political light was Hans Dietrich Genscher, Germany's longtime foreign minister. European-style German liberals favor business and a free market. In 1982, however, the liberals switched their support to the Christian Democrats. (This had little impact on business, as the system functioned regardless of the party in power.)

The 1980s also saw the emergence of *die Grünen*

(The Greens), a group committed to protecting the environment, nuclear disarmament, dropping out of NATO, and slashing defense spending. The Greens lured away young Social Democrats and were a major factor in the SPD's 1982 election defeat and Kohl's success. The Greens' politics struck a chord with the traditional German love of nature; as a result, German manufacturers became more ecologically conscious and recycling became a national concern — more so than in most European countries. The Greens leading figure was Petra Kelly, the daughter of a German mother and an American father. (In 1992, she died in what appeared to be a double suicide pact with her lover, a retired German general.) Other parties quickly jumped on the environmental bandwagon, and the Greens remain a minority group. At one extreme of the political spectrum is the now virtually inexistent German Communist Party (the KPD); at the other are right-wing groups with neo-Nazi overtones.

After reunification, West Germany's national parties (the CDU, the SPD and the liberal FDP) filled the power vacuum left by the demise of the East Germany's communist regime, and the political structure in the larger context remained essentially unchanged.

Business and the unions exert influence on the federal government, as do the regional administrations (*Länder*) through hundreds of registered lobbyists. However, the traditional corporate ploy of winning favors through campaign contributions is largely a thing of the past. A decade ago, a major scandal — in which leading German corporations received massive tax breaks in return for illicit payments to the main parties — scared corporations into cutting back their donations. As a result, political parties now rely largely on government funding.

"Guest Workers"
vs. "Foreign Fellow Citizens"

During the *Wirtschaftswunder* years (Germany's economic recovery in the 1950s), jobs were offered to workers from less affluent European countries. Italians, Yugoslavs, Portuguese and Turks who came flooding in were called *Gastarbeiter* (guest workers); successive German governments saw them as a temporary workforce to meet the country's labor needs of the moment, rather than as immigrants. Many took over jobs that Germans wouldn't do (street cleaning, garbage collecting, janitoring) or found work in factories. All were better off financially than they would have been at home.

Though the economic boom is a thing of the past here, the foreigners keep coming: *Aussiedler* (outsettlers), Russians whose German ancestors emigrated to Russia 200 years ago; any Russian Jews who request entry; refugees from the Balkan war; and, until 1993, a goodly number of asylum-seekers from the Third World. Those who can't find work often sign up for government aid. According to *The Economist*, these many thousands lessen the nation's already suffering coffers by DM3 billion (US$2 billion) annually.

When Germany's economy slowed down, the German government introduced incentive schemes designed to tempt *Gastarbeiter* into returning to their respective countries. Six million of them, mostly Turks, opted to stay put.

Many have lived in Germany for more than 30 years, and their children often speak German exclusively. Neither the Germans nor the Turks themselves are doing much to integrate what amounts to a sizeable ethnic minority living in virtual ghettos, with their own schools, churches, shops and restaurants. They're now officially referred to as "foreign fellow citizens," but few qualify for citizenship. Those who do remain isolated on the margin of society, and few of them exercise their right to vote in German elections. There are no Turkish parliamentarians in the *Bundestag* to speak on their behalf, and no Turkish TV newscasters to remind the general populace of their presence.

While the intermittent attacks on Turks or Turkish property by right-wing "skinheads" are condemned by the leading political parties, the continued presence of these now-unwanted "guests" remains an increasingly contentious issue. The pressure on the Turks has increased since reunification. With nationwide unemployment higher than it's been in many decades, more and more people are questioning why foreigners should be allowed to fill "German" jobs or to collect "German" financial aid.

Ordnung in Cyberspace

Juergen Rütterger, the minister of technology and research, is in the process of drafting Germany's first federal multimedia censorship law, which would make both providers and users liable for content deemed pornographic, violent or racist. In 1996, German authorities briefly closed down a number of pornographic sites on CompuServe, the U.S. Internet provider.

Because Europe's largest multimedia conglomerate — Bertelsmann (now in partnership with AOL and Deutsche Telekom) — is based in Germany, the country is in a position to dominate Europe's Internet scene. Rütterger is lobbying with officials in leading industrial countries to establish an international "code of conduct," which the aforementioned federal multimedia censorship law would implement.

6   The Work Environment

The Work Ethic: West vs. East

A society deservedly proud of its reputation for precision and order inevitably attaches great importance to individual performance, and that starts with proper training. Germany's tradition of corporate apprenticeship dates back to the 14th century, the same era during which Reformationist leader Martin Luther spoke of *Beruf* — the calling to which each person is assigned by God and to which he or she is duty-bound to perform as well as possible. The result is the most highly skilled labor force in the world. Extensive apprenticeship training and retraining programs not only maintain low youth unemployment but are also crucial factors in ensuring quality. Mercedes-Benz AG, to cite one example, put 6,000 managers and workers through a one-year retraining program before building its first S-class model.

In East Germany, however, this commitment to excellence had been undermined during communist rule by poor pay, lack of motivation, inadequate training and overstaffing. At least one East Berlin office building employed a woman full time to water the plants near the elevators on its five floors. An East German hotel manager explained the difference in approach under Communism this way: "Relations with guests in East Germany were completely different. You didn't have to care for the guest. The waiter chose who to serve and it was a privilege to be seated. Today, we [in the east] have to get used to the idea that the guest is king."

Still, compared to the workforces in other communist countries, the East Germans were models of efficiency. But this, too, had its drawbacks. In the unified East European economic system (Comecon), different countries were often assigned to produce different parts of the same product. Thus, while East German factories made locomotive bodies, other communist countries were assigned to produce the wheels, the engine parts, etc. This cumbersome arrangement infuriated the East Germans, as it forced them to slow down in order to keep pace with the slower factories outside their borders.

In 1992, the government launched a campaign to help former East Germany "catch up" to its western counterpart. Subsidized retraining courses, ranging from heavy engineering to hairdressing, were offered. Corporate managers, hotel workers and waiters attended sessions on the importance of such unwritten rules as eye contact, wardrobe, politeness, tact, deodorant and an overall pride in one's work. Today, the work-ethic gap is, in many cases, a thing of the past. Some East German hotels, for example, exceed their western counterparts in efficiency, elegance — and cost.

The Good Life

The 1950s built up the image of the German workforce as determined and hardworking. Today, German workers have the highest net incomes in

Europe. And they put in fewer hours than anyone else in the industrialized world — 1,651 hours a year, compared with U.S. workers (1,907 hours annually) or Japanese workers (2,201 hours annually). Despite recent cutbacks and proposed reforms (loss of four weeks at a health spa every three years paid for by the state; the threat of pension reductions for early retirees, reduced unemployment benefits and sick pay, and possible loss of job protection guarantees), six weeks paid vacation and thirteen months pay a year are still standard in most German enterprises.

Germans are used to feeling secure in their jobs. Unlike American workers, once Germans are hired, they're there for life. But with unemployment rising (to 4.7 million, or 12 percent of the workforce, as of January 1997, the highest since the 1930s), employers are reluctant to continue hiring, as they fear the high cost of benefit contributions and are concerned about being burdened with a large workforce if business declines.

This raises the question: How can a country with the world's highest labor costs and (at least on the surface) least industrious workforce remain a leading exporter of high-quality, competitively priced products? Part of the answer is that the commitment to training pays off: craftsmen and workers are frequently highly skilled. And the expectation of high performance is so ingrained, says one American executive who spent years in Frankfurt, that it's considered the norm. Also, executives tend to have college degrees augmented with specialized courses, and German universities have a strong business and marketing bias.

What Fish Has A Dark Spot?

International polls consistently show Germans

to be less satisfied with their jobs than employees in other major European countries (with the exception of Britain) or in the U.S. This reflects the widespread view that work is, in fact, *Beruf* — an obligation that enables them to enjoy the good life: A nice home, long weekends, travel, sports and a Mercedes are considered the basics.

Initiative is rarely a shortcut to promotion. The route up the corporate ladder is through training, qualification and experience. In terms of the latter, age is a factor. A man of 35 is perceived as someone who is still gaining experience for senior positions. A man in his mid-50s is said to be in his prime. Although job mobility is increasing, it's still common to spend one's entire working career with one company.

To fill a vacant post, an applicant usually has to have successfully completed the requisite courses, whether it be a technical course, a graduate degree or advanced on-the-job training. The Germans have courses for everything, including leisure activities. Getting a German driver's license requires six months of expensive lessons in both driving theory and practice. A would-be fisherman will spend three months at night school preparing for a written test. Sample question: "What fish has a dark spot just behind the first backfin?" There's also a practical test in which the applicant puts together a rod and reel.

Pyramid Hierarchy

The corporate decision-making process is pyramidal, with a handful of professional managers (or sometimes just one person) ruling from the top down. Middle-level managers involved in the groundwork may not even be aware of the final purpose of their efforts. "Despite everything we have done, we remain more hierarchical than the rest of the West," remarked Heinrich Stahl, a professor of cultural and media studies in Berlin. There's much discussion about American-style decentralization of decision making, but so far, it's rarely practiced. Gut reactions and instinctive feelings are mistrusted. Recommendations from below are not usually expected and go unheeded.

At Volkswagen, for example, the Berlin Wall had hardly come down when chairman Carl Hahn announced that VW had signed a joint venture to start producing cars for the new East German market (an opportunity he called "an unimaginable gift of fate"). It was the chief executive's call, and he made it. For the 30 or so years that Hermann Josef Abs was head of the powerful Deutsche Bank, a Bonn economist recalls, "Nobody ever told him what to do."

Middle management's main responsibility is the operational day-to-day overseeing of strategic decisions they've often had little or no say in formulating. Their traditional deference to authority makes this acceptable. To executives used to a more collaborative system, it seems too authoritarian. But one positive side effect of the German system is that it cuts down on staff infighting.

Planning and More Planning

Regardless of the size of the organization, German executives plan for the long term and in detail — and they often criticize U.S. corporate strategies for being shortsighted. Spontaneity is neither encouraged nor appreciated, and risk taking is avoided, though what Germans define as "risk" is often normal market uncertainties in other countries. German banks dominate business and set a very cautious tone; venture capital is virtually nonexistent.

Prior to a launch, market and product testing can sometimes be carried to extremes. At the main Mercedes-Benz plant in Stuttgart, visitors are proudly shown the testing rooms where the doors of a vehicle are hydraulically slammed shut and re-opened again and again for days, until the door finally falls off its hinges. The number of openings and closings is meticulously recorded and compared with previous door slammings to ensure that the component has lost none of its toughness.

Mittelstand: Changing of the Guard

Two-thirds of the workforce is employed by the *Mittelstand* — the thousands of small and medium-sized businesses, often family owned, that are scattered around the country. Many are exporters with world share markets in the range of 80 to 90 percent. Many of the postwar entrepreneurs who founded *Mittelstand* firms are now dying or retiring. It's estimated that by the year 2000, some 300,000 companies will be in need of new owners and that less than half of them will be passed onto younger family members. Moreover, many who *do* inherit are hiring bosses from outside the family.

As a result, changes in management style seem likely in the next few years. Some firms are actually allowing customers to dictate what products will be developed. They're also encouraging teamwork (rather than isolation) between departments, making greater use of outside suppliers, and even considering the possibility of bringing in partners. Foreign management buyouts (with former owners often retaining a minority share) are on the increase.

Women in Business

The Three Ks

Historically, German women were considered inferior (both intellectually and spiritually) to German men, but like Eve in the Garden of Eden, capable of doing great harm. In 18th-century Hamburg, it was considered improper for them to sing in church; they were there to worship, not to be heard. As late as the 19th century, a widow was required by law to have a male guardian for her children, even if she was able to be their sole support, and to let him administer her family property, including what may have been added to it by her own efforts. In 1851, the respected German philosopher Arthur Schopenhauer wrote that women existed "in the main solely for the propagation of the species and were not destined for anything else."

The phrase *"Kinder, Kirche, Kuche"* (children, church, kitchen) sums up their traditional role. To that end, Adolf Hitler dismissed women from government posts, as well as from medical and legal professions in the 1930s, while at the same time offering tax breaks and maternity benefits to those who married and devoted themselves to raising families.

It wasn't until the 1960s that German women were assured the right to own property on their own. In the 1970s, paragraph 1356 of the pre–World War II Civil Code (which defined a German woman's duty as "housework") was finally deleted. The marriage and divorce laws of 1977 established that family roles were to be defined by mutual agreement and protected women's property in case of divorce, which women have the right to initiate.

Current Trends

Though these days women are highly visible in the workplace, the overall picture remains uneven. Until 1994, a married woman could not retain her maiden name in her work. Chancellor Kohl subscribes to the popular view that there's nothing to stop a woman from holding down a job, *if* she can master the logistics of being a devoted wife and mother, too. At work, women often receive lower wages than men, and a low "glass ceiling" limits advancement. According to a 1963 survey, only 3.4 percent of all leading West German executives were female. Today, the percentage remains virtually the same.

Reunification has proved to be a setback for East German working women. Many were dismissed to create places for men who lost their jobs when inefficient factories were closed down. For the women who remained employed, there was both good news and bad. Wages and salaries were higher than under Communism, but instead of equal pay regardless of gender, as before, the women now received less than their male counterparts. Other changes followed. In 1995, militant feminists from former East Germany, where abortion was legal, joined forces with feminists in West Germany, where it wasn't, to try to introduce legalized abortion throughout the "new" Germany. But the German parliament voted against the measure, and abortion was declared illegal nationwide.

Still, some German women have done spectacularly well within the system, among them fashion designer Jil Sander and Beate Uhse, owner of Europe's largest retail sex-oriented products business. In 1994, Jutta Limbach, a former law professor, was appointed Germany's first female chief justice (it's a 12-year position). There are twenty-six women members in the *Bundestag* (roughly 10 percent of the total), more than in any other European parliament, and two women hold office in the senate.

Strategies for Foreign Businesswomen

Interpersonal relations in the German workplace are formal, though not as formal as in Japan, for example. Colleagues who have worked together for years still start the day by shaking hands with each other; and it's still unusual for secretaries and executives to be on a first name basis. Some workers boast that they don't even know the first names of coworkers. However, one result of this formal atmosphere is that it makes it harder for males to become overly familiar with female coworkers or subordinates.

The task-oriented atmosphere at meetings can also be an advantage to women. Business is conducted with the minimum of small talk or other distractions. The thing that matters above all else to German executives in a business meeting is the expertise of their interlocutor or interlocutors, regardless of gender.

The title Ms. has no equivalent in German, and a businesswoman can expect to be addressed as *Frau* or Mrs., whether she's married or not. *Fraulein* or Miss is nowadays used only to address those under the age of 18. So if a woman insists on being addressed as Miss, she should make that clear when she's first introduced or when she introduces herself ("This is Miss So-and-so ..."), and she should consider having the title printed on her card. If, despite all effort, the German side addresses her as Mrs., a correction — even a tactful one — could prove awkward.

Many Germans will shake hands with the males present but will wait until a woman offers her hand to be shaken, so be sure to do so. An older German may kiss a woman's hand. This is not a romantic gesture: it's old-fashioned, formal behavior. Some younger executives may follow suit, particularly those from aristocratic families. If the senior German is an older man, he'll expect to be treated with formality and courtesy by men and women alike.

Incidentally, he's more likely than an American counterpart to still be married to his first wife. In fact, one of the surprises of meeting senior German executives socially is that their wives tend to be the same age as they are, rather than Younger Wife Number Two, or possibly three.

8 Making Connections

Tasks First, Friendship Later

German friendships tend to be deep and highly selective. The same applies to close business relationships. Repeated visits, a few dinners, and a good performance record in the shared business venture should improve and consolidate the connection.

But dealings can remain on a formal basis for years. Unlike many Asian and Latin cultures in which relationships come first and set the tone for business, the German culture is definitely task oriented — focusing on the essentials and advantages of the deal at hand. But while trust may not be as important initially as it is in other countries, once it's lost, it will be difficult to regain.

Like all Europeans, Germans are masters of the quick day-trip to a neighboring country for a business meeting that allows them to be home in time for dinner. Europe's air and rail services are geared to these tight schedules, which leave little time to develop personal relationships or to study the complexities of another culture.

Go-Betweens

Networking across borders is an old European tradition. The 19th-century French statesman Prince Charles-Maurice de Talleyrand (who managed to serve both the monarchy and Emperor Napoleon without skipping a beat) used to receive a fee from both sides after negotiating a treaty between countries. In more modern times, socially connected Europeans (often with titles) have transferred this skill to facilitating business connections and collecting a cut as "consultants."

Modern transport, international business schools, and the European Union have brought European countries closer together, and even in a technological world, "who you know" remains an important factor. As many introductions take place in musty gentlemen's clubs in London, Paris and Hamburg (many of these establishments have exchange facilities), while shooting boar in the Alsace or Buckinghamshire, or in the first class lounge at Heathrow or Fiumicino, as they do in corporate offices and dining rooms.

Most international firms have branches or agents in the Federal Republic who can introduce you to prospective partners. Chambers of commerce and embassies can also help with your initial approach.

But a more focused approach is to enlist the services of a German bank. Though they have a justifiable reputation for being conservative and prefer to place "safe bets" on established businesses in proven fields, they are in a position to provide useful inside information about specific industries and even help with key introductions and important contacts. For example, Deutsche Bank's controlling shareholdings range from 28 percent of Daimler-Benz to 35 percent of the Holzman construction company, and the bank is represented on 400 super-visory boards throughout German industry.

Almost without regard to the nature of the initial approach, you can be sure of one thing: German firms take nothing for granted. Even before your first scheduled meeting, your German interlocutors will have screened your company to determine whether it would be a suitable partner, and they'll have familiarized themselves with what it is you're selling.

Trade Fairs

Participating in an industry trade fair is another excellent way to make business contacts. Three of the world's five largest fairgrounds are here, and they claim to host two-thirds of the top 150 international fairs. New fairgrounds are being built and older ones expanded and upgraded.

Berlin's biennial *Funkausstellung* specializes in consumer electronics; new events (added in 1996) include one for the food and hotel industry and one for kindergartens. Frankfurt hosts (among others) an international car show, the publishing world's most important book fair, and a quality control devices show. Nuremberg has a toy show. Cologne is the site of *Fotokina*, the world's leading photographic equipment fair, plus 39 others. Dusseldorf hosts between 40 and 60 such events annually, including the world's largest fairs for health care, packaging, plastics and confectionery machinery. In 1995, Dusseldorf's *Messe* (exhibition center) headed the country's list with 1.8 million visitors and a turnover of DM450 million. Hanover and Munich weren't far behind.

9 Strategies for Success

Well-Trodden Ground

The global spread of German business is illustrated by the two-decade presence on the Mediterranean island of Malta (pop. 350,000) of a Playmobil factory, which produces plastic toy figures. Bertelsmann (the Hamburg-based media company) has interests in North America, the U.K., Italy, France, Russia and elsewhere. German firms have been active in the U.S., both as exporters and capital investors (and more than 700 American companies have branches or subsidiaries in Germany, with investments totalling US$10.7 billion). Siemens bought out American companies in areas like telephone exchanges and automobile electronics, and Hugo Boss, the fast-growing German clothing group, has also expanded into the U.S. market.

The privatization of East Germany's former state enterprises has opened up a whole new market, but to date, foreign investment remains sluggish. (The U.S. heads the list with 15 corporations, including Coca Cola and Philip Morris.)

Ten Guidelines

1. Your product or service will almost certainly
    require compliance with a host of complex
    (and generally inflexible) regulations. Study
    them carefully. Make sure your product quali-
    fies, or can be made to qualify, before venturing
    further.

    Most Germans are concerned about the envi-
    ronment. (The demand for recycled paper is so
    great that manufacturers have to pulp *new*
    paper to make it.) So if you're selling to Ger-
    man consumers, make sure that your goods
    conform to environmental regulations, which
    are the toughest in Europe.

2. Almost as important as the product itself is
    after-sales service. Your company's reputation
    for such service is likely to be a determining
    factor in the German firm's decision to do busi-
    ness with you. You might want to consider set-
    ting up a service office in Germany.

3. Your German partners will want to establish
    proper lines of communication with your orga-
    nization. As quickly as possible, provide them
    with the relevant names, titles, areas of respon-
    sibility and brief professional biographies of
    staff members with whom they'll be in contact,
    keeping the numbers down to avoid confusion
    and crossed wires. Once these personnel have
    been identified, keep changes to a minimum
    and explain them, should they occur.

4. The Germans will base their actions on the
    signed agreement, and they'll expect their busi-
    ness partners to do the same. In case of a dispute
    or problem, that agreement will be their guide-
    line. If a problem *does* arise, explain it clearly,
    unemotionally and in detail. Spell out what

steps have been taken both as damage control and to ensure that the problem won't occur again. Provide as much information as possible: better to supply too much than too little.

5. Respect delivery dates. In fact, try to beat them. That way, your associates will forgive later slips and problems. If you foresee a delay, give as much advance warning as possible.

6. Though verbal contact may be in English, the Germans are most likely to write to you in their own language, though they won't expect you to reply in German. All promotional materials and instruction manuals should be translated. To avoid bloopers that could cause embarrassment or possibly even give offence, have the German text rechecked by a professional (preferably a German). The Germans tend to use sans-serif typefaces for their printed brochures and materials. Sales literature in a serif font will look foreign to them.

7. Put forward advertising campaigns based on facts, not emotions. "Madison Avenue" advertising may emphasize the glamour or excitement of a product, but a Hamburg ad agency will focus on the reasons why the product is superior. Be aware that the law forbids comparisons with competing products. Case studies and personal testimonials are highly regarded.

8. Arrange for an early exchange of visits by key staff members. Besides providing a detailed and intensive program of business activities for the visiting Germans, plan out leisure activities as well, such as the touring of historical sites. (Unless you're very sure of your ground, avoid theatrical performances that require a fluent knowledge of your language.) Your counterparts will certainly do the same for your staff.

9. Keep all correspondence brief, formal and to the point. Unless told otherwise, address letters to the company ("Dear Ladies and Gentlemen"), rather than to an individual executive.

10. When doing business with German businesswomen, attempts to use flirtation or charm as a substitute for a direct, businesslike approach will probably kill a deal. American business executives are often surprised at the abrupt change of mood once the brief opening pleasantries are over and serious discussion with a female German counterpart begin.

Every presentation or sales pitch is a performance of sorts, but keep yours low key. Let the strength of your proposal speak for itself. Avoid sweeping gestures, dramatic declamations, boasting and jokes. Avoid keeping your hands in your pockets, as this is considered slouching. Above all, avoid keeping your left hand in your trouser pocket while shaking hands with your right. This is considered bad manners.

10 Time

Time Waits For No Man

The Germans are sticklers for punctuality. If a German couple is invited to dinner at 7 P.M., they're likely to arrive early and wait in their car for the hour to strike.

In theory, you're allowed 15 minutes' grace — *das akademische Viertel* — the quarter of an hour that German university students traditionally have to wait for a tardy professor before a lecture is officially canceled. Similarly, in a business situation, if you're a no-show after 15 minutes, your meeting may be called off. And keep in mind that to be even a few minutes late for a scheduled appointment, whether business or social, will be taken as a sign of inefficiency or disinterest.

One advantage of all this is that you're not likely to be kept waiting. (Arrive a few minutes early and you will be received as the hour strikes.) Another advantage is that Germans don't allow themselves to be interrupted. The norm is to concentrate on the task at hand, to the exclusion of all others. Once a meeting has started, you can usually count on your interlocutor's undivided attention.

A Nation of Clockwatchers

With the exception of senior executives (who arrive early and leave late), employees in factories, stores and offices leave promptly at quitting time. Working late is often seen as a sign that the worker can't finish the job in the time allotted to it. Should your business drag on beyond closing time, you'll be very unpopular, and your German hosts will let you know it by pointedly looking at their watches.

Deadlines, German-style

Germans regard deadlines as sacrosanct. Once there's agreement on a date, they take the commitment seriously. To ensure that agreed upon dates (and quality standards) are met, they may ask for penalty clauses (and a warranty) to be built into a contract.

If you're unable to meet a deadline, give your German partners as much advance warning as possible and be clear about the reasons. Above all, don't waffle.

Business Meetings

Arranging the Meeting

Making appointments in advance shows that you're well organized. Two weeks' notice isn't unusual if the meeting is scheduled by fax, longer if a top executive is involved. You have the best chance of getting everyone's undivided attention if the meeting is scheduled between 11 A.M. and 1 P.M. In the afternoon, your German interlocutors might start getting restive as quitting time approaches. Avoid Friday afternoons. Some offices close by 3 P.M., and everyone is anxious to begin their weekend.

It's worth remembering that virtually every German takes at least four weeks vacation a year, generally in July and August. Some factories actually close down during this time (though this is less usual in Germany than in France, Italy or Spain). So check to confirm that your counterpart will be available. Also, little work is done during regional festivals such as Oktoberfest and the Carnival that precedes Lent in Catholic areas.

Send background documentation, spreadsheets and figures in advance, whenever possible. This is particularly important in the case of an introductory

meeting between organizations. If the material is
presented in German, the gesture won't go unno-
ticed. Make sure you're thoroughly familiar with
every aspect of the issues to be discussed, down to
the smallest detail. Have backup charts (they like
visuals) and figures available to illustrate your arguments. Discreetly inquire as to whether the meeting
will be conducted in English, or whether your hosts
will be using an interpreter. In the latter case, it
would be wise to engage one of your own.

Arriving at the Company

Be on time. Arriving even two or three minutes
late will create a bad impression. Most firms have a
conference room for such meetings. The senior visitor should enter the room first, followed by the rest
of his team in order of rank. The Germans consider
themselves polite and expect visitors to recognize
this. They are also protocol minded, and a meeting
will begin with handshakes all round. It's not a bad
idea to ask permission before taking notes.

Identifying Who's Who

Protocol requires that the highest ranking visitor introduces himself, or is introduced, to the
senior manager present, and then the senior manager is introduced to the visiting team — again by
seniority — with brief descriptions of their area of
responsibility. Then it's the German host's turn to
do the introductions. Smiles aren't required. The
senior German manager will be seated in the center,
with the next senior executive on his right.

Business cards are always exchanged before
the start of the meeting; they should provide further indication of who's who on the opposite side
of the table. *Geschäftsfuhrer* corresponds to corpo-

rate president, the top man. *Generaldirektor* is the general manager or managing director, *Finanzdirektor* is the chief financial officer, and a *Direktor* is a senior manager. In addition, the card will include personal titles, such as *Doktor* (used by anyone with a doctorate). Titles of nobility take precedence over professional titles, and you're likely to occasionally met a manager who is a *Graf* (count), a *Freiherr* (marquise) or a *Freifrau* (marchioness).

Don't even think of using first names (most business introductions are, in any case, limited to surnames only). Your hosts are, and will for a long time remain, *Herr* Schmidt, or *Doktor* Schmidt, or *Frau Doktor* Schmidt, or *Graf* Schmidt. It may be years before your German counterpart says, "Please call me Otto."

Common German Business Titles & Their English/American Equivalents

Vorstand	Chief Executive Officer (AG corp.)
Geschäftsfuhrer	Chief Executive Officer (GmbH corp)
Generaldirektor	President or managing director
Bereichsleiter	Division head
Abteilungsleiter	Department head
Gruppenleiter	Group head
Finanzdirektor	Director of Finance

Some Meeting Guidelines

1. The highest-ranking or eldest person usually enters the room first. All things being equal, men enter before women.
2. Your hosts are looking for solid information on

which to base their judgment. Leave out the hyperbole and the "hard sell." Just present the facts as systematically as possible. Also, be prepared for requests for further details. Some of their requests may seem puzzling, but the Germans will have their reasons. When *you* ask questions, avoid a confrontational tone.

3. Germans tend to put more physical space between each other then do Asians, Americans or other Europeans when holding a conversation. Though you may feel uncomfortably far away, don't move your chair in closer. Rearranging the furniture in a German office is considered highly insulting. While an Italian businessman might put his hand on a counterpart's arm or elbow while talking, a German executive would leap away from such a gesture.

4. Expect people to smoke before, during and after the meeting. Germans light up everywhere they please. Hospital waiting areas are notorious for trapping clouds of smoke in often windowless rooms.

5. Unlike the Asian style, in which an exchange of pleasantries serves as an overture, the Germans expect to plunge straight into things without the benefit of jokes, humor, small talk or photos of the kids. After formal introductions, a visitor may find himself launching straight into his presentation.

6. German executives tend to separate their private and professional lives, and they're not likely to volunteer information about their families. Americans should be aware of the fact that, in Europe, they have a reputation for cross-examining people they've just met about such personal details.

There's no direct German equivalent for the expression "small talk" — Germans would be shocked to think that anything they said was frivolous — but some suitable standby topics of nonbusiness conversation include vacations (and how much you need one), sports (Germans are passionate soccer fans), and the U.S. (presidential elections, environmental issues or movies).

7. The German language is low context, and Germans are low-context communicators. Too much gesticulation or volubility will not be received well. Nonverbal cues and signals aren't widely used, and eye contact is so commonplace that it hardly counts as an indication of anything.

    If your voice is high pitched, try lowering it a little. German voices tend to have a deeper timbre than those in the English-speaking world, and a high voice is a disadvantage.

8. Don't expect more reaction than a formal "thank you" at the end of the meeting or presentation. The Germans are likely to leave the room without offering any reaction at all. To start a detailed discussion at that juncture would be considered hasty. Don't look for hints, winks or nudges. If an opinion is expressed, it should be taken at face value. When a German says your proposal is interesting, he's not making polite conversation. He means it.

    Every aspect of a proposed deal will be examined with care; Germans aren't obsessed with immediate results. And they tend to dislike intuitive thinking or trial-and-error methods. Feel free to send a follow-up letter, perhaps repeating points you think need to be stressed, but don't expect it to speed things up. However, once a decision *has* been made, the Germans will stand steadfastly behind it.

9. When the follow-up meeting takes place (assuming that one does), the senior German executive will open the proceedings, and then either explain the company's negotiating position himself or introduce an expert in the field under discussion. The German arguments will be empirically based, backed by figures and detailed information. And they'll expect their response to be studied before receiving an answer.

10. At no time is it good strategy to "trash" the competition, either yours or theirs. German business is nonconfrontational. Comparisons with the similar products and services aren't primary factors in strategic planning. "There is a kind of general attitude that says you should compete on the basis of your own product's strengths, not on the weaknesses of the competition," says Wolfgang Hansen, president of the German Quality Foundation.

11. Open-ended or ad hoc meetings aren't welcome, so it's important to determine in advance how much time will be needed. If you run over into the German executive's next appointment, it's unlikely that you'll be told to wait or to return later. Few Germans are prepared to be that flexible. They like to believe that their schedules are packed to capacity, and whether or not that's the case is irrelevant.

12 Negotiating with Germans

Hard Bargainers

German negotiation goes from receiving information and subjecting it to expert scrutiny to making a decision and signing an agreement. It can be a long and painstaking process. German negotiators will present a unified front. And they'll be watching the way the meeting is planned and organized for clues about your working methods and those of your company. Conflict is seen as dysfunctional and a symptom of being unprepared. Open disagreement among your team members could "kill" the negotiations. Your presentation must not only be thorough, it must be *seen* to be so. Supporting statistics should be used liberally to illustrate points. When citing figures or technical data, it helps to distribute copies or to use slides, so that everyone can follow.

Charts and graphs are a must. It's rare for a German firm not to have its proud collection of charts; companies virtually function based on them. A computerized color video presentation with pie-charts and graphs would be an effective visual aid and would indicate that your firm is computer literate. But avoid the temptation to make it cartoonlike. Germans don't appreciate mixing business with humor; they consider such an approach frivolous.

Discussion is likely to be to the point. Well-briefed executives will ask questions aimed at getting all the necessary facts, and substantive issues will predominate. As one European executive who has spent years doing business in Germany put it, "You don't know what a businesslike meeting really is until you've experienced German negotiators." As most decisions are taken at the highest level, the managerial big guns tend to be brought in early, provided you or your team are sufficiently senior.

While German executives envy American corporate dynamism, flair and flexibility, they're not about to embrace such an approach themselves. They want to be *really sure* that something will work before they get involved. Therefore, they need time to study the pros and cons of a particular project with care.

Be aware that Germans are very good at pushing for concessions, and often at the last minute, so consider holding something in reserve.

Interpreters

Many Germans like to show off their English, but consider it prudent to use an interpreter during serious negotiations. Although there's little risk that your host's interpreter would intentionally try to mislead you, he or she is, after all, a member of their team. It's prudent not to rely on his or her skill alone.

Having an interpreter of your own can be expensive, but it's money well spent, especially in sensitive, high-stakes negotiations. Your interpreter should be multicultural as well as multilingual and able to pick up on feelings and intonations in both languages. Ideally, you should locate an interpreter in advance, but even after you've arrived in Germany, your hotel business center staff can refer you to companies that provide competent interpreters and translators.

Tips on Using Interpreters

1. Establish Guidelines

Before a meeting, plan the mechanics of how you and your interpreter will work together. For example, how long will you speak before pausing for translation? Ideally, you should practice extensively with your interpreter before your meeting. Go over any specialized vocabulary, brief him or her thoroughly, and provide as much written material as possible.

2. Don't Exhaust Your Interpreter

During a meeting or negotiating session, stop every couple of sentences to allow for interpretation, and try to limit each sentence to one main point. Don't begin another sentence before the interpreter has finished translating the previous one. Interpreters need to rest at least every two hours. If negotiations will continue for more than a day, you may need two interpreters. Using an interpreter can stretch a meeting to three times its normal length, so prepare to be patient.

3. Address Your German Counterpart

When using an interpreter, look toward the head of the German team, not at the interpreter. Speak slowly and clearly, and avoid idiomatic and slang terms.

4. Review What's Been Said — Anticipate What's Coming

After a meeting or during breaks, review with your interpreter the main points that both sides have made. Ask your interpreter what he or she observed about the other side's position or behavior. Try to get a feel for the direction in which negotiations are headed, and anticipate what will need to be said later on.

5.   **Emphasize Important Points As They Arise**

Abstract and complicated discussion is seldom directly translatable. An experienced and qualified interpreter tailors translations to reflect your style, level of formality, tone and intended meaning. You can help ensure that important points get across by repeating or emphasizing them and by making certain that your verbal and nonverbal (body language) messages are consistent with each other.

Business Outside the Law

Underground Economy

Until recently, the law-abiding nature of the Germans and the closeness of the unions to various employers' associations discouraged employers from hiring cheap, nonunion labor and dissuaded private individuals from engaging "moonlighting" workers. But the recent removal of border formalities in the European Union has begun to change that situation, as more and more foreign workers enter the country.

There have been press reports of cheap labor being used in the building industry — contractors hire East Europeans (and even British workers) at lower rates than Germans would accept. The catering sector is another area with a growing reputation for hiring waiters and other staff at "bargain basement" wages.

Some employers also blame Germany's overly generous unemployment benefits for creating a favorable climate for a burgeoning underground economy. During a recent German radio broadcast, a restaurant owner complained that he'd been given the names of three out-of-work chefs by the district employment office to fill a vacancy, but none of them even replied to his offer of a job. And why should they? he said. They were better off collecting unemployment while they continued "moonlighting."

Liberal Drug Policies

Germans worry about the rising crime rate, which has doubled in less than 20 years. They complain that lenient judges do little to discourage nonviolent crime, such as burglaries, which have increased almost threefold in the past decade. Still, the overall crime picture remains less troublesome than elsewhere in western Europe or in the U.S. Critics say that Germany's rosy crime figures are partly due to the country's liberal drug policies. Like several other European countries, notably the Netherlands and Spain, Germany takes a tolerant view of the use of so-called soft drugs — marijuana and hashish. Although these aren't exactly legalized, as in the Netherlands, "soft drugs" were effectively decriminalized by a 1994 decision of the German Supreme Court.

But the issue of dealing with drugs illustrates the wide-ranging power of the states to act independently of each other and the Federal Government. Some *Länder* (such as Bavaria and Lower Saxony) continue to take a tough line on drug abuse, but in North Rhine-Westphalia, even the use of small amounts of heroin and cocaine goes unchecked. In Berlin and Frankfurt, you're likely to see junkies shooting up more or less in the open — in the train stations or in certain parks. Berlin's Bahnhof Zoo, the subway station for the city zoological gardens, was long notorious as a haunt for drug peddlers and addicts, though not so much anymore.

Graft and Bribery

Beamte (senior federal and state bureaucrats) who accept as much as a ballpoint pen from an individual or company doing business with the government face possible dismissal and/or jail, and this sets the overall tone for the business sector. Because they're rare, cases of bribery receive wide media attention. Most German executives would be insulted by a bribe, and such an offer could do irreparable damage to a business relationship. Corruption on the scale of the recent *Tangentopoli* case in Italy — in which dozens of leading businessmen were investigated, and some were subsequently indicted for obtaining government contracts through large-scale bribery of officials —would be inconceivable in Germany.

Present Changes and Future Outlook

Germany backs the E.U.'s drive for more openness and honesty in business. At the same time, the Germans have also tightened up their already high ethical standards, particularly with regard to doing business overseas.

14 Names & Greetings

Small children address their father as *Papa* or *Papi* and their mother as *Mutti*. (In fact, mother remains *Mutti* even to grown-up children, though *Papi* may became *Vater*.) Grandfather and grand-mother are addressed as *Opa* and *Oma* by all gener-ations. Grown-ups often call a young boy or teenager *Junge* or *mein Junge* (literally, "my young one"). Small girls tend to be called *Liebling* (or *Schatzi* in the south; both mean "honey" or "sweet-heart." School children and younger coworkers use each other's first names. Children use titles — *Herr*, *Frau*, etc. — when addressing elders, with the exception of close family friends.

A 1994 law abolished double surnames as too cumbersome. Wives can now opt to be known by their maiden name (they couldn't before), or they can adopt their husband's, but not both. Children must also choose. And children's given names must be chosen from a list — which generally excludes non-German names — approved by the municipal authorities.

15 Communication Styles

Beneath their surface politeness, Germans are wary of strangers. This is the combined result of natural reserve, a lack of skill at dissembling, and, among the older generation, a residual unease about the past. For example, to avoid being demonstrative in public, a German will wait until he or she is quite close before greeting you. Only the young or the impolite wave or shout at each other from far away.

To a non-German speaker, Germans often sound brusque or even aggressive. This is due to the guttural sound of the language, its speech pattern monotones, and to the fact that Germans tend to converse in louder tones than almost anyone else. The style is typified by Chancellor Helmut Kohl, who speaks in long, rapid-fire sentences delivered in a rich baritone, monotone voice.

Because Germans believe that content is more important than style, they can be brutally frank. Rarely is there anything to read between the lines, and hardly ever is the conversation so subtle as to be open to more than one interpretation. The plus side of this trait is that they'll never tell you something because they think it's what you want to hear.

Varnishing the truth isn't a German trait, nor is it a trait Germans appreciate in others.

In meetings, it's a good idea to pause at strategic moments and invite questions — and they'll have them. This avoids interruptions and gives you an opportunity to check that you're being understood.

Be aware that German humor doesn't lend itself to taking the *Kultur* lightly. Jokes about the seemingly interminable length of German operas, for example, will not be appreciated.

Public versus Private

German media exercise great self-restraint when it comes to reporting the private lives of Germany's politicians and other public figures. Separations, divorces and extramarital affairs aren't seen as newsworthy unless they have major political implications. When tabloid reporters recently began sneaking more details of politicians' personal lives into their stories, there was an angry reaction, from the media as well as from the politicians themselves. The belief that private and business lives should be kept separate is widespread in Germany, and a clear distinction exists also between business associates and personal friends.

16 Customs

Carnival (Fasching)

This pre-Lent carnival lasts from November through March. It's more a *season* than a holiday, and Germans celebrate it with gusto. The festivities date back to ancient times, when it was believed that the spirits of winter had to be driven out to make way for spring. During *Fasching*, also known as *die Tollen Tage* ("the Crazy Days"), business grinds to a halt and even somber Germans let their hair down ... somewhat. *Fasching*'s three main days are *Weiber Fasnacht* (when women are allowed to cut in half the ties of any man they see); Rose Monday (day of the big parades); and *Fastnacht*, which means "Night of Fasting," but in fact, people eat, drink and carouse wholeheartedly day and night.

Don't think Rio de Janeiro, but there are parades, and evenings are spent making merry at dress balls complete with a king and queen and a cabaret. The dancing ends at midnight, just as Ash Wednesday heralds the start of Lent. In the Rheinland, carnival is in October, and so is Munich's famous *Oktoberfest* — two weeks dedicated to beer-drinking, eating and Bavarian band music.

Christmas

This is one of the country's most important holidays. On *Nikolaus* (St. Nicholas' Day, December 6th), bags of candies are given to both children, adults and coworkers. Bosses sometimes present employees with chocolate *Nikolaus* statues. All, including non-Christians, are expected to greet others with *Frohe Weihnachten* (Merry Christmas) on Christmas Eve and Christmas Day. From then until December 31st, the greeting becomes *Guten Rutsch ins Neue Jahr* (literally, Good slide into the New Year).

Advent is marked by decorating the front door with a wreath. Sometimes, another wreath is placed on the mantelpiece or dining table with four candles on it — one to be lit on each of the four Sundays before Christmas Day. Special Advent calendars with a series of cut-out windows, one to be opened each day until Christmas, are given to children. Most towns have a Christmas market (*Der Weihnachtsmarkt* or *Christkindelmarkt*) in the main square where decorations, candles, toys and seasonal sweets are sold, along with jewelry, cashmere scarfs and the like. (The market in Nuremberg is one of the oldest and grandest in Europe.)

In the Middle Ages, Christmas Eve was devoted to the staging of mystery plays based on the lives of Adam and Eve, with a decorated evergreen representing the Tree of Life from which Eve picked the apple that caused the explusion of the First Couple from Paradise. The tradition of decorating evergreen trees is, in fact, a German one, and it was in Thuringia in the 1880s that glassmakers discovered the technique for blowing glass bells, balls and other ornaments to hang on the boughs. (Today, trees are sometimes still decorated with real, lighted candles.) Another German contribution is the song "Silent

Night, Holy Night." It was composed in 1818 in a small town near Salzburg, Austria — a last-minute holiday collaboration between a priest and a church organist.

In various parts of the country, St. Nicholas is known by different names, including *Weihnachts-mann* (Christmas Man), *Christkind* (the Christ child), Ash Man and Shaggy Goat. He's sometimes accompanied by *Knecht Ruprecht*, a dour, dark-skinned fellow who carries a bundle of switches — a reminder to children to behave.

Stores and offices close at midday on Christmas Eve. In the evening, after a light meal, families gather in their living rooms to sing carols and exchange gifts. In Catholic areas, the evening ends with midnight mass in a local church.

Holiday fare includes *Christstollen* (a bread filled with almonds and dried fruit), *Lebkuchen* (gingerbread), *Rumtopf* (summer fruits that have been preserved in rum, served over cake or ice cream), *Glühwein* (mulled wine), and marzipan molded into various shapes.

Polterabend: The Noisy Evening

An evening or two before a couple marries (in a required civil ceremony, usually in a city hall), they invite a wide circle of relatives, friends, co-workers and acquaintances to a festive party called *Polterabend*. Traditionally, it's held in a tent. (Church weddings sometimes follow the civil ceremony, but a church will marry only members of its congregation.) Along with wedding gifts, guests come laden with ceramic cups, plates and the like to smash on the ground — a pagan ritual originally designed to ward off evil and unhappiness. The bride-and-groom-to-be get to sweep up the mess. Food and revelry follow.

Music and Museums

When it comes to classical music, the country of Bach, Beethoven and Stockhausen lives up to its past. It's not just that you can attend a performance of the great Berlin Philharmonic. Good music is available almost everywhere. Thanks to heavy subsidies at the federal and state level, every major town is able to support an orchestra and a respectable opera company. Munich has three opera houses, one of which was built by "Mad" King Ludwig. Even medium-sized Mainz has its own opera house. Many of today's leading American singers gained valuable experience singing in German opera houses — and quite a few stayed on.

Every major city has more than one museum. Big cities like Berlin, Frankfurt or Düsseldorf offer a wealth of them (Berlin has 150), along with important art galleries and cultural activities.

Many German cities were a heap of rubble at the end of World War II (notably Berlin and Dresden), and there has been large-scale reconstruction. But you can still walk the narrow, winding medieval streets of Nuremberg and visit the famous street fountains in the old quarter of Augsburg, two of the many towns that emerged more or less intact. You can find history in every bend of the Rhine. And there's history of a more tangible sort in every room of Frederick the Great's Palace of Sans Souci in Potsdam (which, miraculously, survived the destruction of World War II), the finest example of German Rococo architecture in existence.

Gift Giving

When invited to dinner at a German home,

always bring a small gift, such as a bottle of wine, candy, flowers, or possibly a book on a subject that will be of interest to your host. The gift of German wine carries the implication that your host's cellar is inadequate; but imported wine, preferably from California, is a safe bet.

Any bouquet should consist of an uneven number of flowers (but not thirteen). Red roses have romantic connotations, and white lilies are for funerals. In northern Germany, heather is often planted on graves; when in that part of the country, make sure it doesn't appear in your flower arrangement.

When it comes to business gifts, avoid any kind of extravagance. A fine pen, cigars, a silver picture frame or a pocket calculator would be suitable, as would a bottle of good quality Scotch whiskey, cognac, *Sekt* (German champagne), *Schnapps* or vintage American wine. Or you could be more imaginative and opt for computer software: a chess game, for example, or an encyclopedia. German computers are compatible with mainstream U.S. and Japanese computers. Perfume or clothing (with the possible exception of a scarf or tie) are regarded as too personal. Such corporate supergifts as a car or a golf club membership would be considered "over the top." A cash gift is likely be found insulting, demeaning or indecent, and it could backfire.

Schrebergarten and Schultuten

For those who have no house or garden of their own, there's the uniquely German custom of *Schrebergarten*. These are small pieces of land, usually inside or at the edge of cities, that can be rented. Urban dwellers who long for a touch of country living often spent their weekends tending plots of flowers, vegetables or fruit.

Schultüten is another uniquely German tradition. These are enormous, brightly decorated cardboard cones filled with candies that are presented to children on their first day of school (to "sweeten" their rite of passage). Typically, the cones are almost as tall as the children themselves.

17 Dress & Appearance

Business Attire

The German business uniform is personified in Chancellor Helmut Kohl's wardrobe of dark suits, white shirts and conservative ties. Rarely is he seen in public wearing anything else. Germans expect their counterparts to dress in the same serious manner, and trendy or flashy fashion statements are best avoided. Germans also see correct posture as a sign of inner discipline.

Businesswomen's attire, though it should also be sober, need not sacrifice elegance — greys, black, pinstripes, worn with perhaps a brooch, or a strand of pearls. Pants are acceptable, but sexy or provocative outfits could not only create a negative impression, but risk trivializing the message.

If the German company happens to be an "alternative" business — media, graphic arts, fashion, computer software development — the dress code will be more relaxed. (These firms are less formally structured and tend to make more collective decisions.) However, this doesn't generally denote a significant change in other aspects of doing business. In fact, it's so hard for Germans to suspend their love of order that the wearing of less formal clothes in "alternative" firms becomes *de rigueur*. Thus, those who come to work in dark suits are considered to be breaking the rule that there should be no rule.

When it comes to casual wear, blue jeans are ubiquitous. In summer, German men often wear sandals.

Ethnic Clothing

Bavaria is one of the few places in Europe where men and women wear their traditional dress to work — a style sometimes called Tyrolean. A female bank teller or secretary in Munich is quite likely to wear a dirndl, an outfit consisting of a white blouse, a tight, laced-up bodice, and a full skirt with an apron over it. Men wear *Lederhosen* (leather or suede breeches, often with suspenders) with woolen stockings. The traditional hat for both sexes is made of grey felt and sports a badger's tail for decoration.

Throughout the rest of Germany, regional costumes abound, though they're usually reserved for festivals and other special occasions. On feast days in the Black Forest, peasant women still wear elaborate, lace-trimmed costumes with headdresses known as *Tracht*. In some towns, brides and grooms marry in traditional local garb. Such clothing can be quite elaborate, including scarves, embroidery, lace, ribbons, frock coats and layered skirts.

18 Reading the Germans

What Body Language?

German body language reveals little. In fact, it's so understated that it hardly qualifies for the name. Just as, in conversation, they come straight to the point without frills, the Germans are very economical with hand gestures and facial expressions. This is not an attempt at oriental inscrutability. Too much gesticulating or grimacing is considered flashy and unnecessary, and smiling during business meetings is regarded as inappropriate.

The Germans do everything front-and-center. They walk straight into a room. They stand straight, legs slightly apart, make eye contact, and extend their hand for a short, firm, no-nonsense handshake. When a German gets to know you better, he's likely to combine shaking your hand with a brisk pat on the back.

Entertaining

Business Meals

It's been said all along that Germans warm to strangers slowly. The real breakthrough on a personal level comes when you're invited home for dinner. But before that happens, your German associate is likely to be your host at a working lunch or dinner at a restaurant. "Power" breakfasts are practically unheard of. Prelunch drinks are served with hors d'oeuvres, followed by a heavy meal. Lunch (eaten between 12:20 and 1 P.M.) is the main meal of the day. The evening meal is traditionally a light affair of cold meats and bread — hence the name *Abendbrot* (literally, evening bread).

When seated at a large table that makes handshaking difficult, Germans may rap their knuckles on the table as a form of greeting. In some restaurants, there's a communal table reserved for regulars, called a *Stammtisch*.

The unwritten rule is to limit the discussion of business to before (briefly) and after the meal. Lunch is an opportunity to tactfully learn something about your host. For instance, though Germans tend to be private, they also tend to be hypochondriacs. If you ask a German the ritual question, "How are you?," he or she may respond with a litany of various and sundry ills. Sports, movies, travel, the arts and, to a certain extent, politics are good conversation topics. Avoid World War II, gossip about other members of either your own or your German counterpart's companies, and religion.

In thanking your host for the lunch, say that you wish to reciprocate, but don't press him to give you a date. Tell him you'll call his secretary to make the appointment. When you return the compliment, a good touch would be to propose choosing a German wine and deferring to your guest about the choice.

"I've Had Pig"

When in doubt about what to choose, don't hesitate to consult your host. If there's an English version of the menu, the translation can be hilariously fractured. Try to conceal your amusement. For all you know, the translation may have been done by the owner's cousin.

To summon a waiter in a restaurant, raise your hand to the level of your head, palm outwards, index finger outstretched until you catch his eye. If you spot someone you know in a restaurant don't wave. Nod your head instead.

In spite of growing concerns over healthy diets, the traditional German cuisine still contains punishingly large doses of fat and carbohydrates. Typical starters are *Boullion mit Ei* (beef boullion with a raw egg whipped in it) and *Leberknodelsuppe* (liver dumpling soup). Seasonal game is a great favorite — wild boar, venison, duck and pheasant. Other main dishes include *Leberkas* (a spongy loaf of ground pork and beef) and various *Braten* (pork) dishes.

The Germans eat an average of 5.5 ounces of pork per person per day, more than any other Europeans. In fact, when someone's lucky, they sometimes say *Ich habe Schwein gehabt* (I've had pig); this custom probably dates back to lean times, when having a pig meant that one's family would be fed.

Schnitzel refers to a *cut*, rather than to a *kind*, of meat, though more often than not, it will be ... pork. *Wurst* is sausage, and Germany boasts some 1500 different kinds, with the main ingredient ranging from beef, veal, pork or chicken to rabbit or horse. The American hot dog is a descendent of the *Frankfurter*, a *Wurst* from the city of Frankfurt am Main. Cabbage (*Kraut*) and potatoes (*Kartoffel*) are ubiquitous. Curly noodles called *Spätzle* (literally, little sparrows) and boiled dumplings (*Klösse*) are also popular.

Spring is *Spargel* time, and asparagus is served with absolutely everything. (There's actually an asparagus museum in Bavaria.)

Eating in a German Home

The invitation is likely to be for 7 P.M., with the meal beginning at 7:30. There will probably be pre-dinner drinks. Gin and tonic is popular, as is Scotch.

Appetizers may include ham, tongue and various sausages, followed by a clear soup. The main course is more likely to be meat than fish — pork and sauerkraut, perhaps, or a beef stew. *Tafelspitz* is a delicious selection of meats and assorted vegetables that have been boiled together and that are eaten with mustards and sauces. Traditionally, each of the different meats is attached to a long string, so that each can be taken out individually and sliced.

Dessert is a big deal. Germans may be stern in some respects, but they do have a sweet tooth. It's not for nothing that the Black Forest lends its name to a rich, cream-laden chocolate cake. And from Austria, the Germans have borrowed *Sacher Torte*, a dark fruit cake encased in chocolate that's invariably eaten with *Schlag* (cream).

After dinner, there's often coffee and a digestive drink such as *Schnapps*, a high-alcohol-content liquor, similar to eau-de-vie, that's sometimes flavored with cinnamon, peppermint, peach or other essences.

A few dining protocols:

- To begin the meal, Germans say *Guten Appetit.* When drinking, they say *Prost.*
- The fork remains in the left hand while eating.
- Don't cut potatoes, pancakes, dumplings or fish with a knife. It suggests that they're tough. Use your fork.

The Ritual of Sunday Lunch

If you're asked to Sunday lunch, you'll be taking part in a typical weekend ritual. The meal is likely be at a country restaurant, with various members of the family present, and will be followed by a long walk in nearby woods or countryside. For this, the Germans will dress down somewhat, but the men will still wear sports jackets and probably ties.

Beer: Liquid Bread

Given a choice, ask to have lunch in a tavern or beer *Keller*. Your host is likely to have a favorite one and will be pleased to show it off. The food will be simple — different kinds of *Wurst*, or pig's feet with cabbage and boiled potatoes. Unlike in English pubs or some American bars, patrons are served at tables, never at the bar. But the real lure is the excellent beer. To draw a tankard of fresh beer so that it has a thick layer of foam can take up to eight minutes.

Beer is so popular that it's sometimes referred to as *flüssiges Brot* (liquid bread). Germany is home to some 4,000 different brands; in fact, one of every three of the world's breweries is in Germany. *Deutsches Reinheitsgebot* (the German Purity Law) was first established in 1516 and hasn't been altered since. (Munich's Lowenbrau brewery dates back to 1383.) *Reinheitsgebot* stipulates that only four ingredients can be used — malt, hops, barley and water.

Today, there are 20 different types of German beer, including *Pilsner* (bitter and light), *Alt* (darker and fruitier), *Weizen* (to which wheat is added), *Maibock* (May beer, dark and malty), *Weihnachtsbock* (made for the Christmas season), *Rauchbier* (smoked), *Berliner Weisse* (sweetened with raspberry syrup) and *Malzbier* (has minimal alcohol).

20   Socializing

A Fairly Closed Circle

In Germany, personal friends tend to include childhood friends, friendships formed at college, and those forged during the 18 months to 2 years of compulsory military service. Rarely are foreigners admitted to this circle. Business and professional associates form part of a wider, less intimate group. Within their own circle of friends, the Germans socialize frequently. They dine out in groups at neighborhood restaurants, often taking in a movie afterward, and they also entertain at home.

"New Wine" & Other Celebrations

Though a highly industrialized country, Germany observes ancient traditions on a large scale. In some southern villages, children still dance around a beribboned Maypole in the square. The end of the Thirty Years' War is still commemorated with a parade in 17th-century costume (the exact date often depends on when the conflict ended in that locality). Every ten years since 1634, the Bavarian village of Oberammergau stages its famous Easter Passion play, with locals playing all the roles.

In September in the Rhineland, the farthest north that wine is produced in Germany, there are parties to taste the first wine of the season. Onion tarts, an ancient local dish, accompany the tasting.

Birthdays (especially landmark birthdays) are often major events — held in a rented restaurant or hall, with toasts, speeches and often a repertoire of well-known drinking songs. So popular are these celebrations that they've all but replaced traditional saint's day festivities.

Soccer: A National Passion

The Germans have clubs and associations for every conceivable activity, whether leisure or professional. There are branches of the Rotary Club, and the Lions Club; there are eating clubs, drinking clubs and a range of organizations covering everything from archery and archaeology to nudism (popular as a reflection of Germans' love of nature).

There's a widespread interest in sports. The third largest team at the Atlanta 1996 Olympics was from Germany. German executives don't share the Asian and American addiction for golf, but the emergence of world tennis stars Steffi Graf and Boris Becker has raised the level of interest in that game.

But soccer is the sport of choice for German males. Saturday morning games between friends — in parks and small neighborhood soccer fields — are ubiquitous. Many also belong to company soccer teams, and large organizations will have more than one team, because so many employees want to play. During the winter-to-spring soccer season, visitors might be invited to watch the local team's weekly game in the *Bundesliga*, the national league. Even if you're not asked, go anyway. The level of playing is high, as evinced by the German national team's consistently good showing in the World Cup series.

A Note on Saunas

Should you be invited to share one, be warned that it's not unusual for German men and women to take a sauna together, with everyone wearing very small towels or nothing at all.

German Cinema

The turbulent Weimar Republic (1919-1933) produced many great German films, including the Expressionist and social realism dramas of the 1920s and the sound films of the early 1930s. Among the most famous are Robert Weine's *The Cabinet of Doctor Caligari,* Fritz Lang's *Metropolis,* Josef von Sternberg's *The Blue Angel* (featuring a pre-Hollywood Marlene Dietrich) and Leni Riefenstahl's infamous Nazi Olympics documentary, *Triumph of the Will.* Ernst Lubitsch and Billy Wilder also began their careers here.

Jewish emigration during the mid- and late-1930s, in the face of Nazi persecution, dealt a terrible blow to Germany's intellectual and creative communities. Today, despite the talents of Werner Herzog (*Kaspar Hauser; Aguirre, Wrath of God; Fitzcarraldo*), Margaretha von Trotta, Rainer Werner Fassbinder (*The Marriage of Maria Braun; The Bitter Tears of Petra von Kant*) and Wim Wenders (*Paris, Texas; Wings of Desire*), German film production amounts to only a handful — 15 features in 1995, compared with 37 in Italy. The last German film to garner international acclaim was *Das Boot* in 1984.

German theater, on the other hand, is alive and well. Dusseldorf, with a population of about 600,000, has productions all year round at the *Schauspielhaus*, comedy and satire at the *Kommödchen* from mid-September to late August, plus a host of other events. Berlin has 14 theaters, 3 of them experimental, plus the famous *Theater des Westens* for musicals and operettas. And the *Volkstheater* (People's Theater) in the northern town of Rostock (population 250,000) has earned international renown.

21 Basic German Phrases

English	German
Yes No	Ja Nein
Good morning Good day Good evening	Gut Morgen Guten Tag Guten Abend
Please Thank you	Bitte Danke
Do you speak English?	Sprechen Sie Englisch?
I don't speak German.	Ich spreche nicht Deusch
What's your name?	Was heissen Sie?
I live in London.	Ich wohne im London.
Excuse me/I'm sorry	Entschuldigung/Verzeihung
How much is ...?	Wieviel kostet?

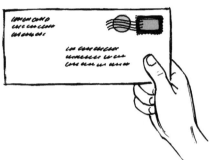

22 Correspondence

The *Deutsche Bundespost* (Germany's Postal Service) requires that business mail be addressed in the following way:

Herrn
Wilhelm Schneider
Bavaria Film GmbH
Goetheplatz 150
80120 MUNCHEN
Bundesrepublik Deutschland

Herrn means Mister and usually occupies a line by itself. If the letter is addressed to a company, the correct term is *Firma*.

Given name. Family name.

Company name with designation, whether GmbH or AG.

Street address, followed by the street number. Had it been a street, it would have been *Goethestrasse*.

Required five-digit postal code. City name (usually capitalized).

If the company has a post box, this follows after the name — *Postfach* 10 03 33. Box numbers are always written in pairs.

Letterheads: More Ordnung

By now you will not be surprised to learn that there is a national standard layout for business letterheads, which is usually observed. After the company name comes its designation, most frequently GmbH or mbH, which stands for *Gesellschaft mit beschrankter Haftung* and is the rough equivalent of Inc. Larger corporations, usually publicly traded, have the letters AG, or *Aktiengesellschaft* (*aktien* being the German for shares). Under the company name there is often a space marked *Datum* (date) and another marked *Betreff* (subject). At the bottom of the page large companies often state their capitalization to indicate how large they are.

When starting a letter addressed to an individual always use personal titles.

23. Useful Numbers

These are local numbers in Germany. If dialing from outside Germany, you must use your country's international access code followed by Germany's country code [49].

- International Access Code from Germany . . . 00
- Long Distance Access Code. 0
- Toll-free Numbers. 0130
- City Codes
  Berlin . . . . (30)
  Bonn . . . . (228)
  Cologne . . . . (221)
  Dusseldorf . . . . (211)
  Frankfurt . . . . (69)
  Hamburg . . . . (40)
  Munich . . . . (80-81)
  Stuttgart . . . . (711)
- World Trade Centers. . . . Bremen (421) 174-660, Hamburg, (40) 37-26-30, Hannover (511) 302-90-50, Leipzig, (341) 211-40-75, Rostock (381) 5-13-95, Ruhr Valley (209) 179-710

Books & Internet Addresses

After the Wall, by Marc Fisher. Simon & Schuster, New York, USA, 1995. An American correspondent's comprehensive portrait of Germany in the immediate aftermath of reunification.

Germany in the Heartland of Europe, by Eleanor H. Ayer. Marshall Cavendish, New York, USA, 1995. A good study of Germany's economic, strategic and political role in contemporary Europe.

The Germans, by Gordon Craig. G.P. Putnam's Sons, New York, USA, 1983. This eminent historian's book is still considered the classic work on postwar Germany. Filled with insight and historical background.

These Strange German Ways, by Irmgard Burneister. Atlantick-Brucke, Hamburg, Germany, 1980. A useful handbook for explaining customs, attitudes and behavior.

Germany and the Germans: An Anatomy of Society Today, by John Ardagh. Harper & Row, New York, USA, 1987 (updated 1996). A longtime expert's explanation of how modern Germany works.

Hitler's Willing Executioners: Ordinary Germans and the Holocaust, by Daniel Jonah Goldhagen. Alfred A. Knopf, New York, USA, 1996. An international bestseller that the *New York Times* described as "masterly" and a "landmark."

Web Sites

General business information site:
http://www.accelon.de/home.html

Data bank of German companies (listed by category, alphabetically and geographically):
http://branchenbuch.com/

German cultural calendar (movies, concerts, exhibitions, etc.):
http://www.welt.de/kultur/welcome.html

German Embassy in Washington D.C.:
http://www.germany/info.org

World Trade Almanac

The *World Trade Almanac* is a first-stop reference encyclopedia for international business people in need of detailed, up-to-date information on the top 100 economies of the world. Each country survey includes a map and information on the country's:

- Economy
- Foreign Trade
- Business Culture
- Marketing & Distribution
- Business Law
- Business Travel
- Contacts

World Trade Almanac
ISBN 1-885073-07-0
844 pages, 100 countries, charts, graphs, and maps

Economic, Marketing, Trade, Cultural, Legal & Travel Surveys for the World's Top 100 Countries

World Trade Almanac
1996–1997

The *World Trade Almanac* also contains detailed articles on International Payments, Worldwide Trade Agreements, the Basics of Importing and Exporting, International Marketing and a Glossary of trade terms.

The *World Trade Almanac* is ideal for importers, exporters, attorneys, bankers, trade consultants, customs brokers, freight forwarders, chambers of commerce and trade missions. Its 844 pages are packed full of difficult-to-find information that will give you a jump start in your dealings worldwide.

Available from your local bookstore or order direct.

WORLD TRADE PRESS®

Professional Books for International Trade

1505 Fifth Avenue
San Rafael, California 94901 USA
Tel: (415) 454-9934, Fax: (415) 453-7980
e-mail: WorldPress@aol.com
USA Order Line: (800) 833-8586